Technology through the Ages

CONSTRUCTION
THROUGH THE AGES

From Pyramids to Plumbing

MICHAEL WOODS AND MARY B. WOODS

TWENTY-FIRST CENTURY BOOKS / MINNEAPOLIS

To Caden Woods

Twenty-First Century Books™
An imprint of Lerner Publishing Group, Inc.
241 First Avenue North
Minneapolis, MN 55401 USA

For reading levels and more information, look up this title at www.lernerbooks.com.

Main body text set in Bembo Std Regular.
Typeface provided by Monotype Typography.

Library of Congress Cataloging-in-Publication Data

Names: Woods, Michael, 1946–author. I Woods, Mary B. (Mary Boyle), 1946–author.
Title: Construction through the ages : from pyramids to plumbing / Michael Woods and Mary B. Woods.
Description: Minneapolis : Twenty-First Century Books, [2025] I Series: Technology through the ages I Includes bibliographical references and index. I Audience: Ages 11–18 I Audience: Grades 7–9 I Summary: "From building brick houses to the Great Pyramids, ancient peoples accomplished great works of construction by developing new technologies and building off ancient building techniques. Discover the science behind the architecture of the ancient world"—Provided by publisher.
Identifiers: LCCN 2023049721 (print) I LCCN 2023049722 (ebook) I ISBN 9798765610107 (lib. bdg.) I ISBN 9798765629918 (pbk.) I ISBN 9798765638934 (epub)
Subjects: LCSH: Building—History—To 1500—Juvenile literature. I Building materials—History—To 1500—Juvenile literature. I Architecture, Ancient—Juvenile literature.
Classification: LCC TH16 .W663 2025 (print) I LCC TH16 (ebook) I DDC 624.09—dc23/eng/20231107

LC record available at https://lccn.loc.gov/2023049721
LC ebook record available at https://lccn.loc.gov/2023049722

Manufactured in the United States of America
1 – CG – 7/15/24

CONTENTS

INTRODUCTION

What do you think of when you hear the word *technology*? You probably think of something totally new. You might think of research laboratories filled with computers, microscopes, and other scientific tools. But technology doesn't only refer to brand-new machines and discoveries. Technology is as old as human society.

Technology is the use of knowledge, inventions, and discoveries to make life better. The word *technology* comes from Greek. *Tekhne* means "art" or "craft." Adding the suffix *-logia* meant "the study of arts and crafts." In modern times, technology usually refers to a craft, technique, or tool itself.

There are many types of technology, including medicine, agriculture, and machinery. This book looks at a form of technology that fulfills some of the most basic human needs. Construction technology provides us with shelter, food, water, transportation, and much more.

From the Ground Up

The first humans on Earth moved from place to place, looking for food. They often built new shelters every time they moved. They used poles and animal skins to make tents. Or they wove reeds together to make huts. The first bricks were made by packing mud into molds and drying them in the sun.

Around 10,000 BCE, humans began to settle in villages and cities. As cities grew, people needed larger, more permanent buildings. People began to build monuments, palaces, roads, and bridges. As cities got even bigger, people needed canals, tunnels, harbors, lighthouses, and sewage systems. Ancient builders learned new techniques and looked for new materials to make new kinds of structures.

Ancient Roots

Ancient peoples developed most of our modern building materials, including concrete, glass, bricks, and tiles. Ancient builders often developed new materials and technology by trial and error. Sometimes they copied and improved on technology used by other cultures. Gradually, ancient builders learned to build bigger, stronger, and more impressive structures.

Many ancient buildings are no longer standing. Archaeologists piece together clues to guess what these buildings looked like. In many cases, ancient peoples wrote about buildings or made pictures of them. So even if a building is gone, modern archaeologists can still learn a lot about it.

CHAPTER ONE

Construction Basics

T he first *Homo sapiens*, or modern humans, lived about three hundred thousand years ago. They lived in small groups and got their food by hunting game, fishing, and gathering wild plants. When the food in one area was used up, the group moved to a new place. These peoples were hunter-gatherers who made tools from stone, wood, animal bones, plant fibers, and clay.

Ready-Made Homes

Some people think that the earliest humans lived in caves, but very few early peoples were cave dwellers. Caves didn't make pleasant houses. They were often damp, dark, and cramped. Sometimes they were already occupied by bats, snakes, spiders, and other wild animals.

But some early humans, especially in cold places, did live in caves. Because their walls were made of thick layers of earth and stone, caves were often warmer than human-built dwellings of the time. Archaeologists have found evidence of ancient cave

These paintings from the Bhimbetka caves in India show men in the act of bow hunting. Although archaeologists are not sure why ancient people painted on cave walls, the images allow a better understanding of what life was like thousands of years ago.

dwellings in many places.

One of the oldest cave dwellings ever found is in South Africa. Archaeologists have found remains of stone tools showing that people lived in the cave anywhere between two million and four million years ago. A cave in central Greece contains the oldest known human–made wall. Discovered in 2010, the wall partially blocks the entrance to the Theopetra Cave. The wall is twenty-three thousand years old.

Build Your Own

Ancient peoples built houses that suited the weather and the landscape. People in warm regions needed buildings with good airflow. People in cold places needed airtight structures that could be heated. Building materials also depended on the environment. The forests of ancient Europe had plenty of timber, so people there built houses out of wood. Farther east, in what is now Ukraine, ancient peoples made houses with mammoth bones and covered them in animal hides.

Go with the Snow

Many early peoples made their homes in cold northern areas. One of these groups, the Inuit, made temporary snow houses called igloos. While modern Inuit no longer live in igloos, they remain an important part of Inuit cultural heritage.

Igloo builders began by outlining a circle in the snow, about 16 feet (5 m) across. Then they cut snow blocks out of banks of drifted snow. They stacked the blocks to build walls, with each ring of blocks slightly smaller than the one below. This technique created a dome shape. The builders packed any gaps in the walls with loose snow. They poked one small hole in the top of the dome to let in fresh air.

Once the dome was complete, builders created a tunnel that served as an entryway. The tunnel trapped cold air and did not allow it to flow inside the house. An animal skin hung between the tunnel and the igloo's interior.

The thick snow walls and animal skin insulation kept cold air out and warm air in. Oil lamps that burned seal oil provided light and some warmth. Temperatures inside an igloo could measure 60°F (15.5°C) or more, even when temperatures outside were below 0°F (-17°C).

Playing It Cool

While ancient peoples in the north developed techniques to make their shelters warm, people in other places wanted to stay cool and dry. Central Africa is hot and rainy year-round. Early peoples there knew how to make light but waterproof huts.

The builders started with thin saplings, which they stripped of their bark and bent to form an arch. They wove a series of sapling arches together to form a domed hut. They used strips of bark or willow branches to tie the saplings

The hard-packed snow of an igloo allowed inhabitants to stay warm even in sub-zero temperatures.

The word *teepee* comes from the Lakota word *thipi*, which means "dwelling." Teepees were widely used by Indigenous groups in the American plains because they were easy to move from place to place.

together into a solid structure. On top of the skeleton of saplings, builders attached a mat of overlapping leaves that acted like waterproof roofing tiles. Some homes had a large front opening to let in air and light, while others had low, tunnel-like entryways.

Moving Day

Hunter-gatherers moved several times a year. In winter they might head to the coast, where fish were plentiful. In summer they might head to the highlands, where they could gather fruits and nuts and hunt small animals. Herders also had to

By Any Other Name

When people hear the term *igloo*, they usually think of snow houses. But the term actually refers to any Inuit house. Ancient Inuit people built igloos out of wood, stone, whalebone, or sod, depending on what materials were available. These houses were permanent structures, designed for long-term housing. Snow igloos, on the other hand, were temporary shelters.

move often, taking their animals to new pastures. Many early peoples took apart their shelters piece by piece and carried them to the new location.

For example, on the Great Plains of North America, some Indigenous peoples lived in teepees. These shelters were made of a frame of wooden poles, propped together to form a cone. The walls were made of twelve or more buffalo skins sewn together with cord made from animal hide. The walls were held up by a frame made from long, thin wooden poles. Tent pegs or heavy rocks kept the skins attached to the ground.

To move a tepee, Indigenous peoples pulled out the tent pegs, pulled off the buffalo skin covering, and pulled down the poles. Then they bundled everything up and loaded it onto triangular sleds called travois. Dogs often pulled the travois to the new encampment.

Monumental

Ancient construction technology provided more than just practical buildings, such as houses and storage sheds. Ancient peoples also built monuments, such as giant statues, to remember important events or to honor leaders or gods.

Easter Island in the South Pacific Ocean is famous for its ancient monuments. The island sits 2,300 miles (3,700 kilometers) west of Chile. Between 1400 and 1600 CE, Easter Islanders carved nearly nine hundred huge stone statues called moai. The statues probably honored the islanders' chiefs or ancestors.

Following a war on the island in 1680, islanders knocked down the moai. Most of them broke. In the late 1900s and early 2000s, archaeologists restored about fifty moai. The archaeologists placed some of the moai in their original positions, looking out over the Pacific Ocean. They placed others in museums. The rest of the moai still lie in pieces around the island.

The statues are figures of people, with giant heads atop torsos. Most are 10 to 20 feet (3 to 6 m) high. A few stand 40 feet (12 m) high. Easter Islanders carved the statues out of soft rock, probably using stone tools.

The average moai weighs about 14 tons (13 t). One of the largest ever erected weighs 82 tons (74 t). Islanders carved the statues at rock quarries and then moved them to ceremonial sites called ahus. In many cases, ahus were several miles from the quarries.

Several modern archaeologists have attempted to move moai to determine how it was done. One team laid a 10-ton (9-t) moai on a giant wooden sled with ropes attached. It took 180 people pulling on the ropes to move the statue. Another research team tried swiveling a moai in the upright position. They attached ropes to the statue's head and base and rocked it from side to side, pivoting the statue forward. Another team used a wooden sled with log rollers underneath. Team members had to constantly reposition the logs to keep the sled moving. But Easter Island has lots of hills and steep terrain, so the log-rolling method probably wouldn't have worked over the long haul. Even after all the studies and experiments, archaeologists still aren't sure how Easter Islanders moved the moai.

More than one thousand complete moai remain on Easter Island. Although they are commonly referred to as heads, the figures have full torsos.

Another Mystery: Stonehenge

One of the biggest mysteries of ancient construction is Stonehenge. This circular stone monument is in Wiltshire County, England. Ancient people built the monument between 2800 and 1500 BCE. Archaeologists have to guess at the original appearance of the monument, because over the centuries, some stones have fallen down or were carted away to build dams, bridges, and other structures.

Archaeologists believe that the original monument was surrounded by a circular ditch and a low wall of earth and stone. Inside stood large blocks of gray sandstone arranged in a circle. Each block was about 13 feet (4 m) high and weighed about 28 tons (25 t). Smaller stone slabs rested on top of the big blocks, connecting the whole circle. Within this circle was another circle made of sixty smaller bluestones. This inner circle held two additional sets of stones arranged in a horseshoe shape, one inside the other. The horseshoes opened toward the northeast.

Some experts think the monument was an ancient religious center. Others think the stones were set up to track astronomical events, such as the summer and winter solstices. Another theory is that Stonehenge was an ancient graveyard. In 2002 and 2003, archaeologists excavated graves near the site dating to around 2500 BCE. Some of the bodies were buried with objects that indicate the dead were people of wealth and status. Another grave near Stonehenge held the bodies of eight or nine people buried together. They might have been workers who built the monument.

We know very little about how Stonehenge was built.

Despite the mysteries surrounding its original purpose, around 20,000 people gather each year to observe Summer Solstice. They watch the sun rise over the Heel Stone, which stands just outside the circle.

People probably created the outer wall by digging up earth using bones, stones, antlers, and their bare hands. But how did they raise the heavy stones into place? Even more mysterious, some of the bluestones came from a mountain range in Wales, 137 miles (220 km) away from Stonehenge. How did ancient people move the stones such a great distance? Archaeologists aren't sure. It remains a mystery.

CHAPTER TWO
The Ancient Middle East

Between 10,000 and 3500 BCE, some ancient peoples abandoned the hunter-gatherer lifestyle. In the Middle East, people began to farm and build permanent villages. One group settled in a region between the Tigris and Euphrates Rivers. The region was later named Mesopotamia. In modern times, it is part of Iraq, Syria, and Turkey.

Mesopotamia was home to a series of ancient peoples, including the Sumerians, Babylonians, and Assyrians. These groups farmed the fertile land along the rivers. They also built towns and big cities. Some of the most common ancient construction technology originated in Mesopotamia.

From Mud to Brick

Mesopotamia had plenty of clay and mud along the banks of the Tigris and Euphrates Rivers. People used these materials to build sturdy and long-lasting houses. Mesopotamian builders used a construction technique called wattle and daub. It began with a simple frame made from long, thin poles or reeds. The builders

The first man-made bricks, found in modern-day Turkey, look very similar to those used in building today.

wove the reeds or poles together to produce a strong skeleton, called a wattlework. They plastered the wattlework with mud or clay, called daub, which hardened in the sun.

Soon the Mesopotamians improved on wattle-and-daub construction. Rather than building whole walls from packed mud and clay, they began to pack clay into small, four-sided wooden frames. The clay dried to create uniform bricks. Builders stacked them to make straight and uniform walls. People in Mesopotamia made sun-dried bricks as early as 6000 BCE.

Better Roofs

Firing and glazing technology improved other ancient building materials. Some were used to make roofs. Many ancient houses had thatched roofs. Thatch is a mat of straw, leaves, or branches bundled together. Steeply sloped thatched roofs allowed rainwater to run off houses quickly. People inside the houses stayed dry.

But thatch can't keep out stinging and bloodsucking insects. It catches on fire easily. Thatch also wears out and falls apart quickly. Homeowners had to replace thatched roofs every few years.

Mesopotamians made a great advancement in building technology when they developed clay roofing tiles. Clay tiles were longer lasting and more waterproof than thatch. Whereas thatched roofs had to be steeply sloped to shed rainwater, tiled roofs could be built at a shallower angle.

Ancient Petroleum

Parts of the Middle East have big underground deposits of petroleum, or crude oil. In modern times, people use petroleum to make many products, including gasoline and asphalt. People in Mesopotamia used petroleum too.

Bitumen is a by-product of petroleum. In some places bitumen oozes out of the ground, sits in pools, and hardens in the hot sun. At the Dead Sea, bitumen sometimes seeps from the seafloor, hardens, and floats on the surface of the water in huge strands.

Mesopotamians used bitumen as a strong, waterproof mortar and coating for walls, sewers, irrigation ditches,

Bitumen is often collected by hand and used to cover roofs or to waterproof boats.

From Pots to Bricks

In the Middle East and other ancient societies, the first pottery makers shaped bowls and jugs out of clay and let them dry in the sun. But sun-dried vessels broke easily and sometimes leaked. Then pottery makers discovered that heating pottery in an oven made it much harder, stronger, and more water resistant than sun-dried pottery.

Around 3500 BCE, brickmakers in Mesopotamia began to fire bricks in ovens. Like fired pottery, fired bricks were hard and water resistant.

In ancient Egypt, pottery makers learned to make pottery even stronger. They melted sand and other minerals onto the surface of pottery during firing. This process created a hard glaze on finished pots.

There were huge advances in construction technology. Ancient builders now had a new material. These bricks were strong. They did not crumble after heavy rains. They also lasted a long time.

and ships. Craftspeople first heated the bitumen to dry up any water it contained. Then they mixed it with substances such as sand, chopped reeds, straw, or powdered limestone. These fillers added thickness and strength, so the mixture didn't run off a wall or other surface to which it was applied. Workers processed bitumen at construction sites and used it immediately while still hot.

Ancient Sanitation

Mesopotamians built indoor toilets thousands of years ago. Mesopotamian toilets were low walls of hardened brick with open seats on top. Toilet floors were coated with bitumen. Inside, toilets opened onto sewer pipes made of rings of fired clay. Sewer pipes were also sealed with bitumen. The pipes carried wastewater to rivers outside of town.

Archaeologists think that only wealthy people in Mesopotamia had indoor toilets. Some Mesopotamian palaces had several toilets lined up side-by-side.

Building to Survive

Ancient town planners designed cities for protection from enemy attacks. City leaders placed important buildings on the tops of hills because hills were easily defended. Most ancient towns were surrounded by high walls with strong gates.

The first city walls were simple structures made from heaps of stone and earth. But builders soon learned to make better fortifications out of brick and stone. Babylon was an ancient city-kingdom in Babylonia. Nebuchadnezzar II, who ruled Babylon from 605 to 562 BCE, fortified the city with two sets of brick

21

> "As they dug the fosse [moat], they made bricks of the earth which was carried out of the place they dug, and when they had moulded bricks enough they baked them in ovens; then using hot bitumen for cement and interposing layers of wattled reeds at every thirtieth course of bricks, they build first the border of the fosse and then the wall itself in the same fashion."
>
> —Herodotus, ancient Greek historian, describing construction of the wall around Babylon, fifth century BCE.

walls. The walls were so wide that several chariots could drive side by side along the top. A moat filled with water surrounded the outer wall. Eight gates allowed people to enter and exit the city. Entrance gates were often the weakest spots in a city wall, so ancient builders took special care to make gates strong and difficult to penetrate.

Terraces

Many Mesopotamian towns included terraces. Terraces are raised mounds of earth or ledges cut into hillsides. Farmers sometimes cut terraces into hillsides to create level ground for planting crops. Some terraces had buildings on top.

To hold the tons of soil and any buildings that might be erected there, terraces needed strong supporting walls. The walls had to be several feet thick and made from brick or stone.

It took an amazing amount of work to build terraces. Archaeologists studied one Mesopotamian terrace and concluded that it contained 14 million tons (13 million t) of earth. It probably took ancient workers ten years to move that much soil.

The Ishtar Gate was one of several entrances that led to the inner city of ancient Babylon.

What a Tunnel!

In Babylon an impressive brick-lined tunnel connected the city's royal palace and its temple. The two sites were more than half a mile (0.8 km) apart, on opposite sides of the Euphrates River. The tunnel allowed pedestrians to cross under the river.

Builders started digging the tunnel around 2180 BCE and finished twenty years later. Archaeologists believe that builders worked during the dry season when the river was very low. Workers used bitumen to waterproof the brick tunnel.

Archaeologists began excavating the Ziggurat of Ur in 1923, and while most of the structure had been destroyed over time, they used ancient descriptions to reconstruct most of it over the last century.

Ziggurats

Mesopotamia was home to many amazing buildings, including temple-towers called ziggurats. Ziggurats were built in tiers where each tier was a little smaller than the one below. People climbed staircases on the outside of a ziggurat to reach a shrine on top. The shrine was a place for worship.

Two ziggurats have become famous. The first is Etemenanki, also called the Tower of Babel, built in the city of Babylon sometime between 604 and 562 BCE. In modern times, all that remains is the tower's foundation. But when the tower stood in Babylon, it had seven tiers. Its base measured almost 300 feet (91 m) on each side. Its exterior was covered in blue-glazed bricks. This tower is famous from a story in the Hebrew Bible. The story tells how ancient peoples wanted to build a tower that would reach to heaven. Archaeologists think that Etemenanki inspired the story in the Bible.

Another famous ziggurat is the Ziggurat of Ur. Ur was a walled city in ancient Sumer (in modern-day southeastern Iraq). Built around 2100 BCE, the Ziggurat of Ur was a temple to the Sumerian god Nanna. It was built like many other buildings in Mesopotamia, with mud bricks sealed with bitumen. In modern times, most of the city of Ur lies in ruins. But the base of Ur's ziggurat is still standing. In the twentieth century, people restored parts of the Ziggurat of Ur, including a grand staircase that once took people to the shrine on top.

One of Seven Wonders

Stories tell of the famous Hanging Gardens of Babylon, which Nebuchadnezzar II built in the sixth century BCE. According to the stories, the terraced gardens seemed to hang from the king's hillside palace. They held a fantastic assortment of plants and animals and had many waterfalls. We know about the gardens only from descriptions of them written many centuries later.

Archaeologists have never found any actual remnants of the Hanging Gardens. Whether or not they ever existed, the Hanging Gardens of Babylon are world famous. In the fifth century BCE, a Greek historian named Herodotus listed the Hanging Gardens as one of the Seven Wonders of the Ancient World.

CHAPTER THREE
Ancient Egypt

Ancient Egypt is famous for its great construction projects. The Egyptians believed that their pharaohs were gods. Pharaohs had enormous palaces, monuments, and tombs built in their honor. They encouraged architects to build massive, awe-inspiring monuments. The most famous monuments from ancient Egypt are giant pyramids.

An Egyptian man named Imhotep was the first engineer and first architect recorded in history. He designed the first pyramid built in Egypt—the Step Pyramid at Saqqâra near the Nile River. This limestone monument has six layers, or steps, each one smaller than the layer below. The Step Pyramid was built around 2650 BCE as a tomb for the pharaoh Djoser.

Archaeologists have found the ruins of more than thirty-five other pyramids along Egypt's Nile River. Three of the most famous were built at Giza, near the modern-day city of Cairo. These pyramids were the tombs of pharaohs Khufu, Khafre, and Menkaure. The pyramids were made of huge blocks of limestone. Unlike the Step Pyramid, they

The pyramid of Djoser is one of the oldest significant stone structures in Egypt. It was originally covered in white stone and could be seen from a great distance.

have sloping sides, with an outer covering of smooth white stones.

The Largest Pyramid

Khufu's pyramid is the largest Egyptian pyramid. Called the Great Pyramid, it contains more than two million limestone blocks. They weigh about 3.5 tons (3.2 t) each. Workers fitted the stone blocks

"It is a most interesting structure, built of immense masses of rock, fixed together with a great deal of art, and seemingly calculated to last an eternity."

—Ida Pfeiffer, Austrian traveler, on visiting the Great Pyramid in the 1840s

Each of the three Great Pyramids at Giza were built by a different pharaoh. The tallest (*center*) was constructed by Khufu; the second-tallest, by his son, Khafre; and the smallest by Menkaure.

together with great precision.

The Great Pyramid once rose to a height of 481 feet (146 m). Over the centuries, some of the upper stones fell off the pyramid. Thieves also stole the white stones that once formed its smooth outer covering. In modern times, the Great Pyramid stands about 450 feet (137 m) high. Each side of the base of the pyramid is 755 feet (230 m) long. Altogether the pyramid covers an area bigger than ten American football fields.

Moving Pyramid Stones

The blocks used to build the pyramids weighed 2 to 5 tons (1.8

to 4.5 t) each. Workers used sleds to pull the blocks from stone quarries to the Nile River. Using rafts, they floated the blocks along the Nile to construction sites.

As a pyramid rose higher, workers built earthen ramps around its sides. As they added more stones to the pyramid, they made the ramps higher and higher. Using sleds and ropes, laborers hauled the big stones up the ramps. When the pyramid was completed, workers tore down the ramps and hauled the dirt away. Archaeologists have identified remains of earthen ramps at several pyramid sites.

Cutting Pyramid Stones

Egyptian stonecutters had a clever way of removing big limestone blocks from stone quarries. They cut narrow grooves into exposed stone or drilled holes with hand drills along a line where they wanted to cut. Next, the stonecutters pounded wooden wedges into the holes or grooves. Then they soaked the wedges with water.

The wooden wedges swelled when wet. After about twelve hours, the wedges began to crack the rock along the cut lines. As the cracks got bigger, the stonecutters inserted larger wedges. They repeated the steps until the slab of rock broke free. Stonecutters in many other ancient civilizations used the same technology.

The ancient Egyptians also used copper chisels, saws, and other tools. These tools were suitable for cutting the soft limestone rock that abounds in Egypt.

Farming Near the Pyramids

Historians believe that the laborers who built the pyramids probably worked on farms most of the year. But during the dry season, when there was little farmwork to do, they built pyramids and other monuments for the pharaohs. Each building project involved about ten thousand workers.

Archaeologists digging at Giza have found traces of the workers who made the pyramids. They have found mud brick tombs holding the bodies of ordinary workers and their families. Larger limestone tombs hold the bodies of supervisors. Archaeologists have studied the skeletons of the workers. Their spines show signs of great stress, indicating that the workers carried heavy loads and did hard physical labor.

Along with the graves, archaeologists have found the remains of settlements where the pyramid builders lived. They have unearthed the ruins of mud brick houses, stone walls, streets, workshops, bakeries, kitchens, storage buildings, and sleeping barracks.

Waterworks

In addition to pyramids, temples, and other monuments, the Egyptians built many practical structures. They built canals for shipping and irrigation, and dams to store water for drinking and farming. They also built sewers and toilets.

What may be the oldest known large dam in the world was built in Egypt in about 2900 BCE. It was built on a wadi, a dry riverbed, southwest of Cairo and made of limestone blocks. The dam reduced the risk of rare flash floods. Water collecting behind the dam also provided water for workers in

This modern illustration shows how the Great Pyramids may have been constructed.

nearby stone quarries.

Like the Mesopotamians, the Egyptians built toilets and drains. Some Egyptian toilets were quite elaborate, with copper drainpipes for carrying away waste. Other toilets were simple stone boxes that had to be emptied by hand. People probably placed clay pots in the bottoms of these toilets to make removing waste easier. Egyptian toilet seats were made of wood or stone.

CHAPTER FOUR
Ancient India

People in western India began settling into villages around 4000 BCE. They built the same kind of wattle-and-daub huts found in early Mesopotamia. Within one thousand years one of the ancient world's greatest civilizations, the Indus Valley Civilization, had emerged in this region. It developed in the fertile Indus River valley and covered an area of around 386,000 square miles (1,000,000 sq. km) in modern-day Pakistan and India.

The Indus Valley Civilization lasted for one thousand years, from about 3000 to 2000 BCE. Then the people abandoned their towns and cities. Experts think that over time, the rivers that Indus Valley people used for water and transportation might have changed course. These changes created floods in some places and left other places without enough water. For this reason, people abandoned their cities for better-watered lands to the east.

Lost and Found

After the Indus Valley Civilization ended, its cities and buildings

The Great Bath at Mohenjo Daro measures 40 feet (12 m) by 23 feet (7 m) and was up to eight feet (2.4 m) deep.

fell into ruin. In some places, new cities sprang up over the ruins. In 1921 archaeologists began excavating two Indus Valley sites, Mohenjo Daro and Harappa.

Archaeologists believe that forty thousand people lived in Mohenjo Daro. Harappa might have had a population of thirty-five thousand people. Archaeologists have also excavated other Indus Valley towns. Several of them were probably as large as Mohenjo Daro.

Town Planning

Harappa and Mohenjo Daro are important because they were among the first cities that used planned construction. Today we call this city planning or urban planning. With city planning, experts decide in advance how to use the land and where to place buildings.

Planners used the same approach for both cities. A huge brick and timber building stood in the center of town. Built on a platform of packed earth and stone and surrounded by high walls, the building served as a protective fortress and government center.

City streets spread out from the fortress in a grid pattern. The main streets ranged from 9 to 34 feet (3 to 10 m) wide. Homes, shops, and other buildings lined the streets.

Homes had solid front walls, with no windows or doors facing the street. This arrangement gave residents privacy and helped protect houses from thieves. Doors were in the backs of the houses. People reached them by narrow paths behind the main streets. The doors often opened into courtyards, where people probably ate and worked in good weather.

Most Indus Valley homes had two stories, high ceilings, and flat roofs. Brick staircases inside the houses led to upper floors and rooftops. Walls were made from big, flat, stacked bricks. The thick brick walls and high ceilings helped keep houses cool in the summer.

Ancient Plumbing

Mohenjo Daro and Harappa had some of the ancient world's most advanced toilets and drains. The city streets were lined with brick sewers. People got drinking and bathing water from underground brick-lined wells. Usually, one well was able to serve an entire neighborhood.

Some houses had bathrooms and toilets. People probably flushed the toilet with a pitcher of water after each use. Waste traveled down a drainpipe to underground sewers that drained into a nearby river.

The bathhouse at Mohenjo Daro was a large brick building with dressing rooms and a central courtyard. The courtyard contained a bathing pool built from clay bricks. Builders added layers of bitumen to make the pool waterproof. Scholars think that people in Mohenjo Daro went into the water to purify themselves during religious ceremonies.

The World's First Dock

The Indus Valley city of Lothal was similar to Harappa and Mohenjo Daro. It was a planned town, with brick buildings, bathrooms, and sewers. Lothal sat on the banks of the Sabarmati River. The river emptied into the Gulf of Khambhat, which is an arm of the Arabian Sea.

People from other Indus Valley towns shipped goods by riverboat to Lothal. From there, boats traveled into the Arabian

The Sabarmati River has changed course, leaving the ancient city of Lothal landlocked. Lothal was once an important stop on a major trade route in the Indus River Valley.

Firing Bricks

Ancient Indian brickmakers stacked clay bricks into mounds that resembled beehives. The brickmakers lit fires underneath the mounds and kept them burning for hours, until the bricks were hardened like pottery. This method allowed brickmakers to harden large numbers of bricks all at once.

Sea. They carried goods west to Mesopotamia, Arabia, and Egypt. In turn, traders from the west sailed to Lothal with cargo. Riverboats then carried the cargo upriver to other Indus Valley cities. The ships carried trade goods such as barley, wheat, cotton, ivory, gold, and timber.

Archaeologists think that Lothal might have contained the world's oldest known dockyards. They have found the remains of a brick structure measuring 122 feet (37 m) by 73 feet (22 m). Built around 2400 BCE, the structure sat alongside the Sabarmati River.

Boats coming downriver or from the Gulf of Khambhat might have sailed into the structure at high tide. Once the boats were inside, a watertight gate kept the water from rushing back into the river. The gate kept water at the same level, so ships were always in line with the dock. A long wharf connected the dockyard to a warehouse.

But some archaeologists question this theory. They think the structure at Lothal might have simply been a large tank for storing water.

CHAPTER FIVE
Ancient China

People in ancient China lived in different kinds of houses, depending on the climate and nearby resources. In many places, ancient Chinese people built wattle-and-daub houses. In wet regions, people built houses on stilts, so their floors remained dry when the ground below was wet. In forested regions, they built houses out of wood.

Some people in northern and northwestern China created cave dwellings by digging into loess cliffs. Loess is a yellowish soil made of fine mineral particles. They sometimes plastered the interior walls of their cave houses with mud and strengthened the roofs with wooden supports.

Rammed earth was another common building material in ancient China. Builders dumped loose wet soil into a hollow wooden frame. They mixed in straw and other substances to strengthen the soil. Builders then pounded down the mixture with heavy poles to make it dense. As the soil dried, it hardened. When builders removed the wooden frame, they were left with a hard earthen wall. They could repeat the process to build the house foundation or sometimes all the

Although less wealthy families lived in smaller houses, ancient Chinese builders employed rammed earth to build all structures, from single-family homes like the one shown here to large multistory dwellings.

walls. Ancient Chinese people used this same method to build defensive walls around their cities and towns.

Keeping Warm

Many ancient Chinese people built pit houses. They dug a shallow hole in the ground and then extended the pit walls upward using wood, mud, or reeds. Pit houses stayed warmer than houses built entirely above the ground, because the earthen walls and floors were good insulation.

To keep people even warmer, Chinese builders invented one of the world's first central heating systems. Builders made houses with raised stone floors, with an empty space between the floor and the ground. Homeowners lit a fire in the space beneath the floor. The heat traveled across the stone to warm the entire house.

Master Builders

The ancient Chinese were skilled carpenters. They learned to fit pieces of timber together to make strong, interlocking joints. They used the mortise and tenon design. In this system, a projecting piece of wood (a tenon) from one beam fits tightly into a hole, a groove, or a slot (a mortise) cut into another beam. Archaeologists have found evidence of mortise and tenon construction in Chinese ruins that date to 5000 BCE.

At first Chinese people covered their homes with thatched roofs. But like builders in Mesopotamia, they eventually learned to make clay roofing tiles. By 100 CE, the Chinese had started to build with clay bricks. Later, Chinese architects adorned buildings with glazed tiles and carved stones.

The Great Wall

The Great Wall of China was the largest construction project of the ancient world. The wall stretches for more than 4,500 miles (7,240 km) across northern China. Ancient Chinese leaders built the wall to protect China from northern invaders.

The Great Wall was not the first border wall in China.

> "This stupendous [structure] . . . has no parallel in the whole world, not even in the pyramids of Egypt, the magnitude of the largest of these containing only a very small portion of the quantity of matter comprehended in the great wall of China."
>
> —British traveler John Barrow, 1804

Other protective walls date to the 600s BCE. In the 200s BCE, Emperor Qin Shi Huang decided to build the Great Wall.

Builders used whatever materials were available nearby to make the wall. They used stone in some parts and rammed earth in others. They always covered the outside and top of the wall with a layer of stone or brick. Construction continued on and off for hundreds of years.

Workers did not build the whole wall from scratch. They connected brand-new sections with walls that were already standing. The wall wound over mountains and through valleys. But it never formed a continuous barrier across northern China. In some places, sections were not connected.

The Great Wall averages about 30 feet (9 m) in height. Its base is about 25 feet (7.6 m) thick, narrowing to about 15 feet (4.6 m) at the top. A paved road runs along the top of the wall. Originally the road allowed workers and soldiers to travel along the wall. The wall contains about twenty thousand watchtowers spaced about 250 feet (76 m) apart.

Most of the original wall collapsed over the centuries. China's government rebuilt some of the wall in the late 1400s and again in the 1980s. In modern times, the wall is a famous tourist attraction.

The Great Wall of China is the longest structure ever created by humans. Builders used sticky rice as mortar on some parts of the wall, and arsenic was used to keep insects from destroying it.

Invasion of the Mongols

The Great Wall of China was an effective defense against small-scale attacks, but it could not keep out Genghis Khan's army. The leader of the Mongol people invaded China between 1211 and 1223 CE. His army entered China through areas where the Great Wall had crumbled or had never been connected in the first place. The Mongols ruled China until 1368.

CHAPTER SIX

The Ancient Americas

N orth, South, and Central America were once home to great ancient civilizations. Few written records remain from these groups, but excavations reveal that ancient American technology was very advanced. Throughout the Americas, ancient peoples built impressive houses, buildings, and monuments.

Mysterious Heads

The Olmec civilization flourished in Mexico between 1200 and 400 BCE. Among the artifacts left by the Olmecs are giant, carved stone heads. Archaeologists have found seventeen heads, most of them at a site called San Lorenzo in southern Mexico.

The heads stand 4.5 to 9 feet (1.4 to 2.7 m) tall. They weigh 8 to 12 tons (7.25 to 10.9 t) each.

They have flat faces, thick lips, and helmetlike hats. Scholars think that the heads were created to honor Olmec rulers.

The heads were carved from basalt, a volcanic rock. Some

Seventeen Olmec Colossal Heads have been discovered in four separate locations in Mexico. Each one has a unique head covering and distinct facial features.

of the heads weigh almost fifty tons (45,400 kg). That's as much as seven fully grown elephants. The rock came from mountains more than 40 miles (64 km) away. Archaeologists don't know how the Olmecs moved such heavy blocks of stone. It probably took hundreds of laborers many months to move the stones into place.

Maya Pyramids

After the Olmecs, other civilizations emerged in Mexico and Central America. The ancient Maya culture flourished between 250 and 900 CE. The Maya built large cities with magnificent stone temple-pyramids, palaces, and monuments. One city, Tikal (in modern-day Guatemala), had a population of around fifty thousand.

The Pyramid of Kukulcán at Chichén Itzá has four staircases, each with 91 steps, leading to a temple at the top where ancient Maya priests performed rituals.

The Maya city of Chichén Itzá (in modern southeastern Mexico) was built in the fifth or sixth century CE. The city is famous for its huge temple-pyramids.

Other Maya cities also had impressive temple-pyramids. Pyramids at Tikal stand more than 200 feet (60 m) tall. Pyramids at Palenque in southeastern Mexico are covered with intricately carved hieroglyphics. Pyramids at Tulum, on Mexico's Yucatán Peninsula, might have been used as astronomical observatories. Scientists have noted how the small windows of the temples line up with certain movements of the sun, the stars, and the planets.

Older than the Olmec

For many years, archaeologists thought the Olmec were the first people in the Americas to live in cities. But archaeologists now think that Caral-Supe, a settlement in Peru, was much older than any Olmec city. They determined that Caral-Supe was founded before 2600 BCE, more than one thousand years before the Olmec. It may be the oldest center of civilization in the Americas.

Water Year-Round

La Milpa was a Maya city in modern-day Belize in Central America. Like many other Maya cities, La Milpa had a huge public square paved with cobblestones. This 4-acre (1.6-hectare) Great Plaza probably served as a marketplace and gathering spot. Archaeologists believe that the square was also a key part of the Maya's water supply system.

The region surrounding La Milpa had few rivers or other permanent sources of water. Water would have been very scarce during the long dry season.

Archaeologists think the Maya caught and stored water that fell during the rainy season. At La Milpa, water ran off the cobblestones of the Great Plaza into a series of drainage canals, dams, and reservoirs. These structures were built from stone blocks and packed clay. They were very effective for gathering and storing water.

Most ancient Maya structures included corbel arches like the one seen here, particularly on important buildings and vaults.

Clever Designs

Maya houses had walls of flat stones layered one on top of another. To make roofs, builders developed a clever design called a corbeled roof. When house walls had been completed to their final height, builders laid another row of stones over the inner edges of the walls. This row reached just slightly into the interior of the building. Then the builders placed another layer of stones and another, each reaching into the interior a bit more. Eventually, the layers met in the center of the house to complete the roof. The roof could not be too wide, or it would collapse under its own weight. But when built correctly, corbeled roofs were very strong and lasted for centuries.

The architectural site at Mesa Verde includes around 600 cliff dwellings. The ancient Pueblo people occupied the area for more than 700 years.

Cliff Dwellings

The ancestors of the modern Pueblo peoples lived in the Four Corners region from the first century CE to about 1300. The Four Corners region is where the borders of the modern states of Colorado, New Mexico, Utah, and Arizona meet. They occupied the Four Corners region of the United States, the meeting place of the modern-day states of Colorado, New Mexico, Utah, and Arizona. Some ancient Pueblo lived in pit houses, with earthen walls and thatched roofs. Others built houses from adobe, or sun-dried bricks.

Some of the most amazing ancient Pueblo construction was built in an area of southern Colorado called Mesa Verde. It is now a national park, but in the 1200s the ancient Pueblo people built incredible houses and other structures high above the ground. Located beneath overhanging cliffs, they look like giant apartment complexes. The towering cliff

47

walls protected residents from the weather, wild animals, and enemies. People had to climb up steep trails, rock-cut stairways, and retractable wooden ladders to reach their houses.

To make their cliff dwellings, the ancient Pueblo people shaped local sandstone into building blocks. They stacked the blocks in layers to make walls. They made mortar from a mixture of soil, water, and ashes. Along with mortar, they also pressed tiny pieces of hard stone between the sandstone blocks. This and a final layer of mud plaster helped strengthen the walls of the dwellings.

Inca Builders

In the 1200s to 1500s, the Inca Empire ruled a vast territory in South America. The empire included parts of present-day Colombia, Ecuador, Peru, Chile, Bolivia, and Argentina. The Inca were skilled builders. When making a wall or building, they cut the stones very precisely. The precision cutting allowed each stone to fit tightly against the ones next to it. This way, the Inca could make structures without using mortar.

The most famous Inca archaeological site is Machu Picchu. This city in the Andes Mountains of Peru is filled with remains that teach us about the Inca's construction technology. There are temples, palaces, stairways, storehouses, burial grounds, irrigation channels, and agricultural terraces. All the buildings were carefully crafted from stone. Archaeologists think the city was a royal estate for Inca rulers.

A vast network of roads and bridges connected different parts of Inca territory. In some places, the bridges spanned vast river gorges. Inca builders used simple technology to

Machu Picchu contains around 150 separate buildings and more than 100 flights of stairs. The stones are so precisely cut and placed that there is not even space for a knife blade between them.

make bridges that were both long and strong. First, they wove long ropes out of plant fibers. Then they braided many ropes together to make thick cables. Five cables formed the framework of the bridge, two for handrails and three for the bridge floor. Bridge builders attached the five cables to stone supports on both sides of the gorge.

Builders wove shorter cables to connect the handrails and the floor of the bridge. They attached pieces of wood to the floor cables to create a solid surface for walking. They attached more wood and branches along the side cables to create walls. Inca bridges swayed in the fierce winds that sometimes blew through river gorges, but they were strong enough to hold people and animals. To keep the bridges safe and strong, local people replaced most of the fiber cables each year.

CHAPTER SEVEN

Ancient Greece

People still marvel at ancient Greek buildings and copy their designs. Athens was a great center of learning, art, and culture. One of the city's most famous sites was its acropolis. An acropolis is a group of temples, theaters, and government buildings on a hill overlooking a city. Many Greek cities had acropolises. But the acropolis in Athens was the most spectacular. It eventually became known throughout the world as the Acropolis.

The Acropolis in Athens has some of the ancient world's most famous architecture. One building is the Parthenon, built between 447 and 432 BCE. This temple honored Athena, the Greek goddess of warfare, wisdom, and arts and crafts. Athena was also the patron goddess, or protector, of Athens. Columns framed the elegant Parthenon on the outside. A magnificent gold and ivory statue of Athena stood inside the temple. In modern times, the temple stands in ruins, but many of its columns and architectural features are still intact.

First constructed as a military defense, the Acropolis later became a central location of religious and academic significance.

Construction Becomes a Science

Built in the 500s BCE, the Temple of Artemis at the city of Ephesus (in modern-day Turkey) was one of the Seven Wonders of the Ancient World. It is remembered for its 127 columns, lined up in perfect rows. Each column was about 60 feet (18 m) tall.

Greek architects used formulas to design temples. These rules told architects what kind of columns to use and how many were needed. The formulas also told them how big the columns should be and how much space to leave between them. Even with the formulas, Greek architects used their own creativity in the details.

Greek builders had a good reason to use so many columns when building with stone. Stone is heavy and it will crack if

At the time of its construction, the Pharos of Alexandria was one of the tallest buildings in the world. Only two of the three great pyramids of Giza were taller.

it doesn't have enough supports along its length. It took a lot of support to keep the stone slabs from breaking under their own weight. Without lots of columns, these stone temples would have collapsed.

Construction became more of a science in ancient Greece. Builders became engineers who used math in designing structures. This allowed the Greeks to build more elaborate structures. They could calculate the weight a slab of stone could hold before cracking. They knew how to space columns correctly. Too few and the stone slabs above would crack. But builders didn't want to space columns too close together either. Columns were very expensive to carve and assemble. Using too many columns was a waste of money.

The World's First Lighthouse

Lighthouses help warn ships away from dangerous rocks and guide them safely into port through fog, darkness, and other hazards. The first known lighthouse warned sailors of dangerous sandbars off the port of Alexandria in Egypt.

Alexandria was founded by the Greek general Alexander the Great after he conquered Egypt in 331 BCE. Alexander was born in Macedonia, north of Greece, and became one of the world's best military leaders.

Called the Pharos of Alexandria, the lighthouse at Alexandria was among the Seven Wonders of the Ancient World. It was built in the third century BCE and named after the island of Pharos, just off the city's coast, where it was built. Construction of the Pharos lasted from 283 to 246 BCE. The lighthouse was 384 feet (117 m) tall. At the top, a giant bonfire was visible far out to sea and warned sailors of the sandbars. A statue of Zeus, king of the Greek gods, may have stood at the top of the lighthouse. Strong earthquakes in the 1300s damaged the Pharos, and it fell into ruins.

Weight Lifters

In some Greek buildings, such as the Erechtheum, columns were carved in the shape of human figures. Columns shaped like female bodies are called caryatids and were named for Greek priestesses. Those shaped like male bodies are called atlantes after Atlas, an ancient Greek god who held up the sky on his shoulders.

Giant Statues

Two ancient Greek statues were also on the Seven Wonders list. They were the Statue of Zeus at Olympia and the Colossus of Rhodes.

Like other ancient cultures, the Greeks often built giant statues to honor gods. The people of Olympia had a temple to honor Zeus. But they also wanted a statue of Zeus inside the temple. About 430 BCE, they hired a sculptor named Phidias to create the statue. Phidias's statue was 43 feet (13 m) tall. It had an inner framework of wood, covered by sheets of metal and ivory. The figure of Zeus was seated on a throne studded with precious stones. People traveled great distances to worship at the temple. Viewing platforms even let visitors climb up and inspect Zeus's face.

"Even lying on the ground it is a marvel. Few people can get their arms around its thumb, and the fingers are larger than most statues."

—Roman writer Pliny the Elder, describing the toppled Colossus of Rhodes, first century CE

The Colossus of Rhodes stood in the Greek port city of Rhodes, on the island of the same name. It was a giant statue of Helios, the Greek god of the Sun. A Greek sculptor named Chares of Lindos designed the statue. Construction began in 294 BCE and continued for twelve years. The statue had an iron framework covered with sheets of bronze. By building a spiral earthen ramp around the statue as they worked, laborers were able to reach the figure's upper portions. The completed statue was 110 feet (33 m) high. It stood for about fifty years, until an earthquake in 226 BCE knocked most of it down.

Tricking the Eye

Seen from a distance, the Parthenon's marble columns and other architectural elements appear straight and perfectly proportioned. But some of these elements were deliberately out of proportion. Greek architects knew that perfectly even buildings, when viewed from certain angles, appear crooked and uneven.

For this reason, Greek architects made the Parthenon's end columns a little thicker than its central columns. That way, they all appeared equal from a distance. Architects spaced the end columns closer together than the central columns for the same reason. All the columns bulge a little at the center, but they look perfectly straight from a distance.

The architectural style of the Parthenon, from its towering columns to its prominent rectangular pediments, has influenced the design and construction of thousands of buildings around the world.

CHAPTER EIGHT
Ancient Rome

A ncient Rome began as a small city around 900 BCE. Over the following centuries, the ancient Romans built a large empire. It began in their home base of Italy. By the first century CE, it reached all the way to north to the border of Scotland and through central Europe, the Middle East, and northern Africa. Throughout their empire, the Romans constructed impressive bridges, roads, and buildings.

The Romans made great buildings by borrowing construction technology from other civilizations and then improving on it. From the Greeks, the Romans borrowed the idea of magnificent public buildings. From the Etruscans, who came before the Romans in Italy, the Romans borrowed the arch. The Romans also developed an important construction technology of their own—concrete. With concrete the Romans could build huge domes, long bridges, and giant stadiums.

The ancient Romans approached architecture as both an art and a science. Many Roman architects learned their craft from a book called *De Architectura* (On Architecture). Marcus

The Pantheon's dome was the largest in existence for more than a thousand years, and remains the largest unsupported dome in the world. It has remained intact as a result of the high-quality mortar and concrete used to construct it.

Vitruvius Pollio, a Roman architect and engineer, wrote the book around 27 BCE. *De Architectura* dealt with all aspects of construction, including building materials, flooring, construction of temples and other public buildings, and even the education of architects.

A Concrete Breakthrough

Ancient people had been using forms of concrete and cement for thousands of years. Concrete is a mixture of sand, stone, water, and paste. The paste—the cement—holds the ingredients together and hardens the mixture into a rock-like material.

Around 600 BCE, the ancient Greeks began using a reddish-brown ash from volcanic eruptions as the paste. It made a stronger form of concrete. However, the ancient Greeks did not use their concrete very widely.

57

Ancient Roman builders may have learned about this new paste from the Greeks. They named it pozzolana because large deposits existed near the city of Pozzuoli. The Romans used cement extensively. They became master builders with concrete and cement. Concrete revolutionized building in ancient Rome. It made construction faster, easier, and cheaper. Roman workers could quickly pour concrete walls that would have taken years to build from brick.

To make concrete walls, builders filled hollow wooden molds with wet concrete. After the concrete hardened, workers tore down the molds. This method allowed builders to create new architectural elements, including domes for roofs. The Pantheon, a famous temple in Rome, had a huge concrete dome. The dome measured 142 feet (43 m) across. It is still standing in Rome today.

Raising the Roof

An arch is a curved structure that spans an opening. Arches are strong. Unlike the flat stone slabs above doorways and walls in ancient Greek temples, arches don't collapse under their own weight. Instead, the downward force of gravity pushes the stones together, making the arch stronger. The simplest arches span doorways and windows. A series of arches set against one another can be used to cover a rectangular space. This kind of ceiling is called a vault. Domes are also based on the arch design. A dome covers a circular or square space. The Romans were the first ancient people to make widespread use of arches in building.

Building Better Bridges

The Romans realized that arches were perfect for building strong bridges. The arch's two legs rested on each riverbank. The curved, upper part of the arch supported the roadway over the river. The two legs on the riverbanks carried the weight of the arch, the road, and the travelers on the bridge.

The Romans built arched bridges throughout their empire. A single arch could span a small river. To make longer bridges, Roman engineers built several arches end to end across rivers, supporting a long flat road above them. Underwater supports kept the legs of the arches in the middle of a river from sinking into the soft mud of the river bottom. One of the most impressive Roman arched bridges is the Alcántara Bridge. Built between 104 and 106 CE, the bridge consists of six stone arches. It still carries cars and trucks across the Tagus River in Spain.

Ancient Stadium

The Colosseum is a giant amphitheater in Rome. The modern building is partially in ruins. But for almost two thousand years, it was the biggest arena in the world. The oval structure was 620 feet (189 km) long, 513 feet (156 km) wide, and 157 feet (48 m) high. Its outer walls were made from a series of arches placed end to end.

Construction of the Colosseum began around 70 CE and continued for ten years. Builders used brick and concrete to make the walls. They covered the outside of the building with stone. Other ancient amphitheaters had to be dug into cliffs or hillsides, which supported the walls. But the

From the Greek word *amphitheatron*, meaning "theater in the round," the Colosseum is the largest amphitheater in the world and has influenced the design of hundreds of modern sports stadiums.

Colosseum is freestanding.

The Colosseum seated more than fifty thousand spectators. From its marble seats, spectators watched fights between multiple gladiators or between gladiators and wild animals. Sometimes the Romans even flooded the Colosseum for mock battles between ships.

Big City, Big Buildings

The city of Rome was the capital of the Roman Empire. At its peak in the first century CE, it was home to one million people. This big city had tall apartment buildings. Some were six or seven stories high. Architects tried to outdo one another by creating taller and taller buildings.

The Roman emperor Augustus, who reigned from 27 BCE to 14 CE, wanted to make Rome a magnificent city to rival the splendor of ancient Greece. Augustus had many old buildings restored and ordered new ones to be created. The new buildings included the Temple of Mars Ultor, dedicated to Mars, the Roman god of war. It was built around 2 CE. This imposing structure featured dozens of caryatids and gleaming white marble inside and out.

Let the Sun Shine In

Window glass was one of the greatest advances in construction technology. Before glass, people covered windows with paper, cloth, or animal skin. This often made it dark inside. Rain, snow, bugs, and birds sometimes came through those windows.

Historians think the ancient Egyptians were the first glassmakers. They were making glass vessels by about 1500 BCE. The Phoenicians, based in modern-day Lebanon, were master glassmakers. They learned to shape and manipulate melted glass by blowing on it through a tube. The first window glass was probably made from a bubble of blown glass opened into a flat sheet.

Roman glassmakers improved upon the glassmaking technology of the Phoenicians. Before Roman glassmaking, only the rich could afford window glass. But as glassmaking became more widespread, glass became cheaper. By the first century CE, window glass was common in many Roman towns. In cooler climates, more people were likely to have window glass.

The Romans probably made window glass by casting, or pouring molten glass into smooth molds. Most windowpanes were about 12 by 24 inches (30 by 60 cm), although some were much bigger. One windowpane from the Roman city of Pompeii was 40 inches (102 cm) long, 28 inches (71 cm) wide, and 0.5 inch (1.3 cm) thick.

Built to Last

By 117 CE, the Roman Empire had reached its greatest size. It stretched from Great Britain in the north, south to northern Africa and Egypt, and east to the Tigris and Euphrates Rivers of the Middle East. To connect parts of this vast empire, the Romans built 50,000 miles (80,000 km) of roads.

The oldest and most famous Roman road was the Via Appia, or Appian Way. Started in 312 BCE, this road led from Rome to the city of Tarentum, Italy. Builders later extended the road to the Adriatic Sea on Italy's eastern coast. The road was more than 350 miles (563 km) long and 35 feet (11 m) wide.

Roman roads were built to last. Each road had a sturdy foundation, up to 5 feet (1.5 m) thick. The foundation was made of layers of packed earth, stone blocks, broken stone, sand, and other materials. Workers paved the roads with blocks of cut stone.

Roads through rainy areas had surfaces that sloped from the top, with the roadsides a little lower than the center. This shape, called a camber, let rainwater drain off the side of the road quickly, so it didn't soak in and damage the pavement. Most Roman roads also had curbstones and drainage ditches at the sides.

Roman roads remained the best in Europe for centuries, long after the fall of the Roman Empire. In modern times, parts of the Via Appia are still in use.

Aqueducts

An aqueduct is a bridge-like structure that carries water, usually over a valley or other gap. The Romans were the ancient world's greatest aqueduct builders. Eleven aqueducts carried water from mountain streams and springs into the city of Rome. Engineers built other aqueducts throughout the Roman Empire.

Some Roman aqueducts were underground channels. Others were aboveground structures. They looked like long arched bridges with channels for carrying water on top. The tallest aqueduct in the Roman Empire is still standing. It is the Pont du Gard in Nîmes, France. Built between 40 and 60 CE, it stands 162 feet (49 m) high.

Aqueducts sloped slightly so that gravity could pull the water through the channels to its destination with no need for pumps. Rome's aqueducts brought about 97 million

Roman emperors Augustus, Caligula, and Trajan ordered the construction of hundreds of miles of aqueducts throughout the Roman Empire. Some are still functional and continue to supply water to parts of modern-day Rome.

Arcs of Triumph

Several Roman emperors created triumphal arches in their own honor. These arches were more decorative than practical. They were carved with words and images honoring the emperor's deeds. The Arch of Constantine was just one of many triumphal arches in the city of Rome. Still standing, it measures 69 feet (21 m) high, 84 feet (26 m) wide, and 24 feet (7 m) deep. It commemorates Emperor Constantine's victory over his rival Maxentius at the Battle of Milvian Bridge in 312 CE.

gallons (367 million l) of water to the city each day. The total system covered 260 miles (418 km). The water flowed into big distribution tanks. Then it traveled through pipes into buildings, fountains, toilets, and sewers.

Plumbing and Heating

A few wealthy Romans had private toilets in their homes. But most ordinary Romans washed at public bathhouses and used public toilets.

Public restrooms contained fifteen or twenty square stone toilets, lined up against walls. A drainage system beneath the toilets carried waste into city sewers.

Roman public baths were community centers as well as recreation areas. They had facilities like those found in a modern-day spa, including swimming pools, steam rooms, and gymnasiums. In addition, Roman baths had gardens, dining rooms, libraries, meeting rooms, and other facilities.

The Romans built baths all over their empire. An underground hot spring fed the baths in Aquae Sulis, England (the modern city of Bath). The baths at Caracalla, Italy, were some of the most impressive. Marble seats, fountains, and statues filled them. Beautiful mosaics adorned the floors and walls.

The Romans heated public baths, homes, and other buildings with hypocausts. These were the same kind of central heating systems as those of ancient China. Hot air from a furnace circulated under the floors, warming the rooms before escaping through a pipe in the roof. The furnace usually burned charcoal or wood.

Tunnels

From 41 to 52 CE, Roman builders produced a masterpiece of ancient engineering. They dug a 3.5-mile (5.6 km) underground tunnel. The tunnel drained water from Lake Fucinus in central Italy and channeled it into a nearby river. Once the lake was drained, Romans used the dry lakebed for farmland. It took thirty thousand workers ten years to build the tunnel.

Roman tunnel builders usually didn't dig rock; they burned it. They used a technique called fire quenching. They heated the rock with fire and then cooled it quickly with water. The fast cooling process caused the rock to crack. Once the rock cracked, workers could remove it easily. They hauled away the rock, built another fire, and repeated the process as the tunnel grew.

Roman builders preferred to build tunnels in very hard rock that was able to support the walls of the tunnel. That way, workers didn't need to line tunnels with brick or stone.

CONCLUSION
After the Ancients

Ancient civilizations rose and fell. Often civilizations grew politically or economically weak, and stronger groups conquered them. But even after a civilization died out, its technology often remained. Conquering groups built on the knowledge of conquered peoples to further develop technology.

After the fall of the Western Roman Empire in 500 CE, Europe entered a period called the Middle Ages. People used to call this time the Dark Ages. People thought the lights went out on science, art, and learning in Europe during this time. But historians say that this is a myth. Progress in technology did slow down, but it didn't stop. There were still builders and engineers, and construction technology advanced in many ways during the Middle Ages. For instance, people used the technology of the arch to build enormous cathedrals across Europe.

The Renaissance began about the 1300s when Europeans took a renewed interest in classical learning, arts, and technology. It lasted through the 1600s. Not only did

The city of Pompeii was covered in almost 20 feet (6 m) of volcanic ash for centuries. The ash preserved the city's structures, artwork, artifacts, and even the remains of many of its residents, giving archaeologists a glimpse into Roman life in 79 CE.

Europeans explore brand-new ideas in art and culture during the Renaissance, but they also looked to ancient Greece and Rome for inspiration. In the 1400s, Italian scholars discovered and reprinted Vitruvius's *De Architectura*. European architects used the old book as a guide. They built structures using domes, vaults, columns, and other features straight out of ancient Greece and Rome. *De Architectura* was the most important book of its kind for hundreds of years.

Neoclassicism

In the mid-1700s, archaeologists rediscovered the ancient Roman cities of Pompeii and Herculaneum. The cities had been buried for more than one thousand years beneath a thick layer of volcanic ash. The eruption of Mount Vesuvius had destroyed the cities in 79 CE. When archaeologists began to excavate the cities, they set off a new wave of interest in Roman architecture. European architects copied designs of buildings uncovered by the excavations.

Architects took a renewed interest in ancient Greek buildings as well. They worked in a new building style called neoclassical. Neo means "new," and classical refers to the culture and art of ancient Greece and Rome.

Neoclassicism began in Europe but soon moved to the United States. US architect Henry Bacon studied the Parthenon carefully and used it as a model for his most famous structure, the Lincoln Memorial in Washington, D.C. The memorial was built between 1915 and 1922.

Still Going Strong

The Theater of Epidaurus in Greece was part of a religious sanctuary dedicated to Asclepius, the Greek god of healing. Ancient Greeks came to the theater to see plays by Aeschylus, Sophocles, and Aristophanes. People also came to hear music and poetry contests. Built against a hillside, the giant, semicircular stadium could hold thirteen thousand theatergoers.

Greek people used the theater for more than one thousand years. Eventually, though, it was abandoned. Winds and rainstorms filled the stadium with dirt and mud. Plants grew over the newly deposited layers of earth. Finally, the stadium was completely buried and forgotten.

Then, in 1881, a Greek archaeologist began to unearth the stadium. Archaeologists found that the stage building had collapsed, but the stage and the seats seemed as good as new. Excavators were pleased to discover that the theater had excellent acoustics.

In 1954 twentieth-century Greeks began staging ancient Greek dramas at the theater. People have continued to stage these plays into the twenty-first century. Every summer, thousands of visitors arrive for the Epidaurus Festival. They watch classic Greek dramas and can feel themselves transported back in time.

Old and New

Ancient construction technology still builds and sustains our modern world. Look closely at any road. You will see that the sides slope down from the center. This is the same camber design used in ancient Rome to drain rainwater. We still use a form of concrete similar to that first used by the Romans thousands of years ago. The arch and the dome are other examples of the past's contributions to the present.

People sometimes combine ancient and modern construction technology. Ancient rammed earth construction has found a new life in combining soil with additives that increase its strength. We call this cement-stabilized rammed earth construction.

By using the same technologies perfected over centuries, humans have continued to improve the buildings they live and work in. Though modern buildings won't last for centuries, we build them faster and make them higher, stronger, and more comfortable for occupants than anything ancient architects could have imagined. Every bridge, building, and other structure fashioned by humans today owes a debt to discoveries made in the ancient world.

TIMELINE

ca. 10,000 BCE — People in the ancient Middle East begin to settle into villages.

ca. 6000 BCE — People in Mesopotamia begin to build with sun-dried bricks.

ca. 3500 BCE — Mesopotamians begin to fire clay bricks in ovens.

ca. 2800–1500 BCE — People in Great Britain build Stonehenge.

ca. 2100 BCE — Workers build the Ziggurat of Ur.

500s BCE — Workers build the Etemenanki ziggurat, which might have inspired the biblical story of the Tower of Babel.

Workers build the Temple of Artemis at Ephesus in modern-day Turkey.

447–432 BCE — Ancient Greeks build the Parthenon.

294–282 BCE — Greek workers build the Colossus of Rhodes.

283–246 BCE — Workers build the Pharos of Alexandria.

200s BCE — Building begins on the Great Wall of China.

ca. 27 BCE — Roman architect Marcus Vitruvius Pollio writes *De Architectura*.

70–80 CE — Roman workers build the Colosseum in Rome.

ca. 500 — The Roman Empire falls to invaders.

1200s — People in the Four Corners area of the southwestern United States build cliff houses at Mesa Verde.

1300s — Europe enters an era called the Renaissance, a time of renewed interest in learning, art, and culture.

Earthquakes damage the Pharos in Alexandria.

1400s — Italian scholars discover and reprint Vitruvius's *De Architectura*.

1400–1600 — Easter Islanders carve almost nine hundred statues called moai.

mid-1700s	Archaeologists begin to excavate the Roman cities of Pompeii and Herculaneum, which had been buried by eruptions of Mount Vesuvius in 79 CE.
	European architects begin to work in the neoclassical style.
1881	Archaeologists begin to excavate the Theater of Epidaurus.
1915–1922	Workers build the Lincoln Memorial in Washington, D.C., whose design is based on the Parthenon in Athens, Greece.
1921	Archaeologists begin excavating the Indus Valley sites of Harappa and Mohenjo Daro.
1954	People begin staging ancient Greek dramas at the Theater of Epidaurus.
2001	Archaeologists date Caral, Peru, to 2600 BCE and determine that it is the oldest city in the Western Hemisphere.
2002–2003	Archaeologists find burials at Stonehenge dating to around 2500 BCE.
2010	Archaeologists find a twenty-three-thousand-year-old stone wall at the Theopetra Cave in Greece.

GLOSSARY

acoustics: the ability to transmit sound for distinct hearing

acropolis: a fortified section of an ancient Greek city, containing temples and government buildings and located on a hill

adobe: bricks made of sun-dried earth and straw

aqueduct: a canal, a pipe, or a bridge-like structure used to carry a large amount of flowing water

arch: a curved architectural structure used to span an opening, such as a doorway

archaeologist: a scientist who studies the remains of past human cultures

architecture: the art and science of designing and building structures

artifact: a human-made object, especially one characteristic of a certain group or historical period

bathhouse: a building with facilities for swimming and bathing

bitumen: a by-product of petroleum, used as waterproof mortar in ancient times

camber: a design in which a road's surface slopes down at the sides

column: a pillar that supports a roof or a ceiling

concrete: a hard, strong building material made by mixing certain minerals with water

corbeled roof: a roof made of layers of stones or other material. Each layer projects farther into the interior of the building than the one beneath it, until the two sides of the roof meet.

dome: a large hemispherical (resembling half a ball) roof or ceiling

glaze: a hard, glossy outer coating on fired pottery or bricks

hunter-gatherers: people who obtain their food by hunting, fishing, and gathering wild plants

insulation: any material that blocks the flow of heat, keeping warm air and cold air separate

monument: a stone or structure built to honor a person or event

mortar: a substance such as cement that seals the spaces between brick, stone, or other building materials

pit house: a house built partially underground, so that the earth forms the lower part of the house

pyramid: a massive structure with a square base and triangular walls that meet at a point at the top

terrace: a series of ledges cut into a hillside or a raised mound of earth. People often create terraces to farm hilly countryside.

thatch: a mat of straw or other plant material used as a roof

tier: a level or a layer

vault: an arched roof that resembles a half barrel or a half tunnel

wattle and daub: a method of building homes using a framework of poles or reeds covered by mud

SOURCE NOTES

22   Herodotus. *Herodotus*. bk. 1 and 2, trans. A. D. Godley. London: William Heinemann, 1920, 223.

27   Ida Pfeiffer, "A Visit to the Holy Land, Egypt and Italy," Project Gutenberg, 2004, http://www.gutenberg.org/files/12561/12561.txt (April 22, 2010).

40   John Barrow, "Travels in China," Project Gutenberg, 2009, http://www.gutenberg.org/files/28729/28729-8.txt (April 11, 2010).

54   Chilvers, Ian. *Oxford Dictionary of Art*. Oxford: Oxford University Press, 2004, 162.

SELECTED BIBLIOGRAPHY

Adkins, Lesley, and Roy A. Adkins. *Handbook to Life in Ancient Rome*. New York: Facts on File, 1994.

Clark, Ronald W. *Works of Man*. New York: Viking, 1985.

Wilkinson, Philip. *The Visual Dictionary of Buildings*. London: Dorling Kindersley, 1992.

Cox, Reg, and Neil Morris. *The Seven Wonders of the Ancient World*. Philadelphia: Chelsea House Publishers, 2001.

Fagan, Brian M., ed. *Discovery!: Unearthing the New Treasures of Archaeology*. New York: Thames and Hudson, 2007.

———. *The Seventy Great Inventions of the Ancient World*. London: Thames and Hudson, 2004.

Feuerstein, Georg, Subhash Kak, and David Frawley. I*n Search of the Cradle of Civilization*. Wheaton, IL: Quest Books, 1995.

Glancey, Jonathan. *Architecture*. New York: DK Publishing, 2006.

Ingpen, Robert, and Philip Wilkinson. *Encyclopedia of Ideas That Changed the World*. Surrey, Great Britain: Dragon's World, 1993.

James, Peter, and Nick Thorpe. *Ancient Inventions*. New York: Ballantine Books, 1994.

Oates, David, and Joan Oates. *The Rise of Civilization*. New York: Elsevier Phaidon, 1976.

Oliver, Paul. *Dwellings: The Vernacular House World Wide*. New York: Phaidon Press, 2003.

Raeburn, Michael. *Architecture of the World*. New York: Galahad Books, 1975.

Saggs, H. W. F. *Civilization before Greece and Rome*. New Haven, CT: Yale University Press, 1989.

Stevenson, Neil. *Architecture*. New York: DK Publishing, 1997.

White, K. D. *Greek and Roman Technology*. Ithaca, NY: Cornell University Press, 1984.

FURTHER READING

Books

Castaldo, Nancy F. *Buildings that Breathe: Greening the World's Cities*. Minneapolis: Twenty-First Century Books, 2023.
Around the world, architects are working with environmentalists to construct new buildings that work with their environment instead of against it. From vertical farms to high-rise forests, discover the new buildings that are transforming our cities.

Kenney, Karen Latchana. *Folding Tech: Using Origami and Nature to Revolutionize Technology*. Minneapolis: Twenty-First Century Books, 2021.
Discover how the ancient art of paper folding is inspiring today's technology and architecture in this in-depth look at the math and history behind folding technologies.

DK. *The Architecture Book*. New York: DK Publishing, Penguin Random House, 2023.
Learn about architecture around the world through this accessible visual guide. This introduction to architecture explores building technologies and styles throughout history, from ancient wonders to Gothic cathedrals to modern skyscrapers.

Woods, Mary B and Michael. *Machines through the Ages*. Minneapolis: Twenty-First Century Books, 2025.
Throughout history, people have used six basic machines to raise up buildings and monuments. From the wheel to the deadly Claws of Archimedes, learn about the history of machines and how they build and destroy.

Websites

Explore the Pyramids
> http://www.nationalgeographic.com/pyramids/pyramids.html
> This website from National Geographic magazine offers a detailed guide to Egyptian pyramids.

How to Build an Igloo
> https://www.pbs.org/wgbh/nova/ancient/igloo-101.html
> If you live in a snowy place, you can build your own igloo. This web page from PBS tells you how.

Mesa Verde
> http://www.nps.gov/meve/index.htm
> This website from the US National Park Service introduces the people who built the ancient cliff dwellings at Mesa Verde, describes the modern-day national park, and offers special links for young readers.

Roman Bath
> http://www.pbs.org/wgbh/nova/lostempires/roman/
> This website is a companion to the NOVA television film Roman Bath, part of the Secrets of Lost Empires series. This site takes visitors on a tour of a typical Roman bath. It also explores the aqueducts that brought water to cities in the Roman Empire.

INDEX

ABOUT THE AUTHORS

Michael Woods is a science and medical journalist in Washington, DC. He has won many national writing awards. Mary B. Woods is a school librarian. Their past books include the fifteen–volume *Disasters Up Close* series and many titles in the *Seven Wonders* series. The Woodses have four children. When not writing, reading, or enjoying their seven grandchildren, the Woodses travel to gather material for future books.

PHOTO ACKNOWLEDGMENTS

franck metois/Getty Images, p. 7; Bettmann/Getty Images, pp. 9, 10, 31; Micheline Pelletier/Getty Images, p. 13; Matt Cardy/Stringer/Getty Images, p. 15; Nik Wheeler/Getty Images, p. 17; Yves GELLIE/Getty Images, p. 19; DEA/A. DAGLI ORTI/Getty Images, p. 20; HUSSEIN FALEH/Getty Images, p. 23; -/US ARMY/AFP/Getty Images, p. 24; Universal History Archive/Getty Images, p. 27; Nick Brundle Photography/Getty Images, p. 28; DEA/W. BUSS/Getty Images, p. 33; SAM PANTHAKY/Stringer/Getty Images, p. 35; Jon Arnold Images Ltd/Alamy, p. 38; Forrest Anderson/Getty Images, p. 41; DEA PICTURE LIBRARY/Getty Images, p. 43; Jimmy1984/Getty Images, p. 44; Design Pics Inc/Alamy, p. 46; Joe Amon/Getty Images, p. 47; ERNESTO BENAVIDES/Getty Images, p. 49; Archive Photos/Stringer/Getty Images, p. 51; Print Collector/Getty Images, p. 52; Roger Viollet Collection/Getty Images, p. 55; Ed Freeman/Getty Images, p. 57; Smartshots International/Getty Images, p. 60; Tim Graham/Getty Images, p. 63; Frédéric Soltan/Getty Images, p. 67. Design elements: AnK_studio/Shutterstock; Ezhevika/Shutterstock.

Cover image: by Ruhey/Getty Images